U.S. PRESIDENTS

CHECKERBOARD BIOGRAPHY LIBRARY

The United States Presidents

ULYSSES S. GRANT

ABDO Publishing Company

BreAnn Rumsch

visit us at
www.abdopublishing.com

Published by ABDO Publishing Company, 8000 West 78th Street, Edina, Minnesota 55439.
Copyright © 2009 by Abdo Consulting Group, Inc. International copyrights reserved in all
countries. No part of this book may be reproduced in any form without written permission from the
publisher. The Checkerboard Library™ is a trademark and logo of ABDO Publishing Company.

Printed in the United States of America, North Mankato, Minnesota.
012009 082012

Cover Photo: Getty Images
Interior Photos: Alamy pp. 9, 29; AP Images pp. 12, 21, 28; Corbis pp. 5, 10; iStockphoto p. 32;
    Library of Congress pp. 11, 13, 15, 16, 19, 20, 25, 27; National Archives pp. 18, 23;
    North Wind p. 17

Editor: Megan M. Gunderson
Art Direction & Cover Design: Neil Klinepier
Interior Design: Neil Klinepier

Library of Congress Cataloging-in-Publication Data

Rumsch, BreAnn, 1981-
 Ulysses S. Grant / BreAnn Rumsch.
    p. cm. -- (The United States presidents)
 Includes index.
 ISBN 978-1-60453-453-5
 1. Grant, Ulysses S. (Ulysses Simpson), 1822-1885--Juvenile literature. 2. Presidents--United
States--Biography--Juvenile literature. 3. Generals--United States--Biography--Juvenile literature.
4. United States. Army--Biography--Juvenile literature. I. Title.

 E672.R86 2009
 973.8'2092--dc22
    [B]
                                                              2008033508

CONTENTS

ULYSSES S. GRANT

Ulysses S. Grant was the eighteenth president of the United States. Before he was president, Grant served in the U.S. Army. He helped the Union win the American **Civil War**.

The **Republican** Party chose Grant to run for president in 1868. He easily won the election. As president, Grant passed a law to make American currency more stable. He also supported adding the Fifteenth **Amendment** to the U.S. **Constitution**.

In 1872, Grant was reelected. He faced problems in his second term. During this time, there were many **scandals** among his party members.

Grant left the White House in 1877 after two terms as president. In his final years, he and his family traveled around the world. Then, Grant returned home and wrote his **autobiography**.

Grant tried his best to lead the country. Yet his reputation as president suffered. However, Grant will always be remembered for his courageous military career.

TIMELINE

1822 - On April 27, Hiram Ulysses Grant was born in Point Pleasant, Ohio.

1843 - Grant graduated from the U.S. Military Academy at West Point in New York.

1846 - The Mexican War began; the army sent Grant to Mexico to fight.

1848 - The Mexican War ended; on August 22, Grant married Julia Dent.

1861 - Grant trained volunteers to be Union soldiers in the American Civil War; in June, Illinois governor Richard Yates made Grant colonel of the Twenty-first Illinois Regiment; in August, President Abraham Lincoln promoted Grant to brigadier general of volunteers.

1862 - On February 16, Grant won the Battle at Fort Donelson; he was promoted to major general of volunteers; Grant won the Battle of Shiloh on April 7.

1863 - Confederate soldiers surrendered to Grant on July 4 at the Battle of Vicksburg.

1864 - Grant was promoted to lieutenant general of all the Union armies.

1865 - Confederate general Robert E. Lee surrendered to Grant on April 9, marking the end of the Civil War.

1869 - On March 4, Grant became the eighteenth U.S. president.

1870 - The Fifteenth Amendment became part of the U.S. Constitution.

1872 - Grant was elected to a second term as president.

1875 - Grant signed the Specie Resumption Act.

1877 - In May, the Grants departed on a trip around the world.

1885 - Ulysses S. Grant died on July 23.

DID YOU KNOW?

✦ Ulysses S. Grant's oldest son, Fred, visited him while he was at war. Fred was 13 when he saw his father fight the Battle of Vicksburg.

✦ Grant was the first West Point graduate to become president. Dwight D. Eisenhower is the only other West Point graduate to become president.

✦ The salary of the president doubled from $25,000 to $50,000 during Grant's time in office.

✦ Grant's Tomb is the largest mausoleum, or aboveground tomb, in North America.

YOUNG LYSS

Hiram Ulysses Grant was born on April 27, 1822, in Point Pleasant, Ohio. Everyone called him Lyss. When Lyss was one year old, his family left Point Pleasant. They moved to a farm in Georgetown, Ohio.

Lyss's father, Jesse Root Grant, was a **tanner**. His mother, Hannah Simpson Grant, was a homemaker. Lyss was the oldest of six children. He had two brothers named Samuel and Orvil. He also had three sisters named Clara, Virginia, and Mary.

When he was about five years old, Lyss began his education. He attended a one-room school in Georgetown. Lyss enjoyed mathematics. He could quickly solve problems in his head.

By the time Lyss was eight years old, he had a job. He hauled wood with a horse and cart. Within a year, he earned enough money to buy his own horse. Lyss

FAST FACTS

BORN - April 27, 1822
WIFE - Julia Dent (1826–1902)
CHILDREN - 4
POLITICAL PARTY - Republican
AGE AT INAUGURATION - 46
YEARS SERVED - 1869–1877
VICE PRESIDENTS - Schuyler Colfax, Henry Wilson
DIED - July 23, 1885, age 63

8

loved working with horses. He sometimes trained horses for farmers. And, Lyss often drove people to and from Georgetown in a carriage.

At home, Lyss helped on the farm. He also helped his father with the **tanning** business. But he did not like this work. So, Jesse asked Lyss what he wanted to do. Together, they decided Lyss should continue his education.

Lyss's birthplace in Point Pleasant, Ohio

WEST POINT

In 1838, Grant attended the Presbyterian Academy. It was about ten miles (16 km) from Georgetown. Grant already knew many of the lessons taught there. So, he did not enjoy the classes.

Grant's father then decided to send him to college. He got Grant appointed to the U.S. Military Academy at West Point in New York. Grant was not happy with this idea. He did not want to be a soldier. But, Jesse made him go anyway.

In 1839, Grant started school at West Point. School officials thought his name was Ulysses

Grant was an average student. He graduated from West Point in the middle of his class.

10

Simpson Grant instead of Hiram Ulysses Grant. From then on, he went by Ulysses S. Grant.

As a West Point **cadet**, Grant studied mathematics and science. He did well in his classes. However, he did not study hard. Instead, Grant spent much time reading books of his own choosing.

West Point cadets also practiced military skills, such as horse riding. Grant was good at handling the horses. In fact, he was the best horseman in his class.

Grant graduated from West Point in June 1843. After graduation, Grant received his first assignment. He became a **brevet** second lieutenant in the Fourth U.S. **Infantry**. This infantry was stationed at Jefferson **Barracks** near Saint Louis, Missouri.

A BRAVE SOLDIER

At Jefferson **Barracks**, Grant served with Frederick T. Dent. Grant and Dent had been roommates at West Point. Dent's family lived near Jefferson Barracks. They often welcomed Grant into their home. There, he met Dent's younger sister Julia.

Julia Grant

Julia and Grant both liked horses and rode together often. They also enjoyed reading poetry to each other and taking walks together. Julia and Grant quickly fell in love.

In 1844, the army stationed Grant in Louisiana. Soon after, he returned to Saint Louis to visit Julia. Grant and

12

Julia became engaged. But before they could marry, the army sent Grant to Mexico.

The Mexican War began in 1846. Mexico did not like that the United States had **annexed** Texas. The two countries also disagreed about the border between Texas and Mexico.

During the war, Grant fought

For nearly two years, Grant fought bravely in the Mexican War.

in battles that led to the fall of Mexico City. He received two promotions for his bravery. By the end of the war, he had become a **brevet** captain.

FAMILY MAN

The United States won the Mexican War in 1848. Grant then returned to Saint Louis and married Julia on August 22. Two years later, the Grants had their first child. They named him Frederick. They would have three more children named Ulysses Jr., Ellen, and Jesse.

In 1852, the army sent Grant to the Pacific Coast. He had to leave his family behind. The next year, Grant was promoted to captain. But he grew unhappy with his job, and he missed his family. So in 1854, he quit the army and returned to Missouri.

Back home, Grant tried to farm. He struggled for four years before quitting. In 1859, Grant joined a **real estate** company. He was not suited to the business. So in 1860, Grant moved his family to Galena, Illinois. There, he worked in his father's leather shop.

Mr. and Mrs. Grant (right)
and their children

A CIVIL WAR HERO

As the Grant family settled in Galena, the nation faced serious problems. The Northern and Southern states disagreed about slavery. The South thought each state should have the right to allow slavery. The North wanted to end slavery in all states.

In 1860, Abraham Lincoln was elected president. He wanted to end slavery. So soon after the election, seven Southern states left the nation. They formed the **Confederate States of America**. On April 12, 1861, Confederate soldiers attacked Fort Sumter in Charleston, South Carolina. This began the American **Civil War**.

Abraham Lincoln was president from 1861 to 1865.

The Northern states were known as the Union. Lincoln called for volunteers to fight for the Union. Grant organized Galena's volunteers and trained them to be Union soldiers. Meanwhile, four more Southern states joined the Confederacy.

16

The Battle at Fort Donelson was the Union's first major Civil War victory.

In June 1861, Illinois governor Richard Yates made Grant colonel of the Twenty-first Illinois **Regiment**. In August, Lincoln promoted Grant to brigadier general of volunteers. Not long after, he received command of all the troops of southeast Missouri.

Grant's troops attacked Fort Donelson in Tennessee. The **Confederates** surrendered to Grant on February 16, 1862. Grant's success at Fort Donelson made him famous. He was then promoted to major general of volunteers.

195

Executive Mansion,

Washington, February 29, 1864.

To the Senate of the United States

I nominate Ulysses. S. Grant, now a Major General in the Military service, to be Lieutenant General in the Army of the United States.

Abraham Lincoln

conto
March 2

President Lincoln ordered Grant's promotion to lieutenant general. Grant was the first American to hold this rank since George Washington.

On April 6, 1862, **Confederate** soldiers started the Battle of Shiloh. It took place at Pittsburg Landing in Tennessee. Thousands of Union soldiers were killed, wounded, and missing. Grant won the battle the next day, but the heavy losses hurt his reputation.

Before the end of the year, Grant and his soldiers moved toward Vicksburg, Mississippi. There, they fought Confederate troops in spring 1863. The Confederate soldiers finally surrendered on July 4, 1863. Grant's victory badly weakened the Confederacy.

In November 1863, Grant and his troops went to Chattanooga, Tennessee. There, they rescued Union troops that were surrounded by **Confederates**. This victory added to Grant's fame. In March 1864, Grant was promoted to lieutenant general of all the Union armies.

Throughout 1864, Grant led Union troops into many bloody battles. More than 17,000 Union soldiers died at the Battle of the Wilderness in May. In June, 6,000 Union soldiers died at the Battle of Cold Harbor. People began calling General Grant "Grant the Butcher."

Still, Grant continued with his plans. In June 1864, he led Union soldiers to Petersburg, Virginia. The fighting there lasted nearly a year. During this time, other Union troops attacked Georgia and the valley of Virginia.

Grant at Cold Harbor

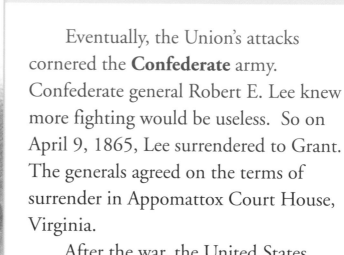

Eventually, the Union's attacks cornered the **Confederate** army. Confederate general Robert E. Lee knew more fighting would be useless. So on April 9, 1865, Lee surrendered to Grant. The generals agreed on the terms of surrender in Appomattox Court House, Virginia.

After the war, the United States entered a time called **Reconstruction**. President Lincoln planned to bring the North and the South together peacefully.

Sadly, Lincoln was **assassinated** on April 14, 1865. Vice President Andrew Johnson then became the new president. Johnson took over the plans for Reconstruction.

Later that year, Johnson asked Grant to tour the South. Grant reported back to

Like Grant, General Robert E. Lee was a West Point graduate.

20

Johnson about conditions there. Then in August 1867, Grant temporarily served as Johnson's **secretary of war**.

The **Republicans** admired Grant's work in the **Civil War** and the national government. So in 1868, they nominated him for president. **Speaker of the House** Schuyler Colfax was selected as his **running mate**. The **Democrats** nominated Horatio Seymour and his running mate, Francis P. Blair Jr. Grant easily won the election.

General Lee and General Grant met at the McLean House to discuss the terms of surrender.

PRESIDENT GRANT

Grant took office on March 4, 1869. He was just 46 years old. At the time, he was the youngest president in U.S. history.

Later that year, President Grant stopped two **financiers** from attempting to control the U.S. gold market. Jay Gould and James Fisk purchased large amounts of gold. This forced the price of gold to rise. Gould and Fisk planned to sell the gold back for a large profit.

The rising price of gold caused a financial panic on September 24. So, Grant ordered the U.S. **Treasury** to sell some of its gold. This stopped the panic. Still, the **economy** suffered.

President Grant also worked to get the Fifteenth **Amendment** approved. In 1870, the amendment became part of the U.S. **Constitution**. This new law gave African American men the right to vote. However, some Southerners tried to keep them from voting. So, Grant passed four Force Acts.

SUPREME COURT APPOINTMENTS

WILLIAM STRONG - 1870
JOSEPH P. BRADLEY - 1870
WARD HUNT - 1873
MORRISON REMICK WAITE - 1874

22

These laws protected the **constitutional** rights of African Americans.

During the **Civil War**, **Confederate** ships had done much damage to Union ships. The Confederate ships had been built in England. So, Grant asked England to pay for the damage. The two countries signed the Treaty of Washington on May 8, 1871. This led to a later decision that England would pay the United States more than $15 million.

Congress passed the Fifteenth Amendment in 1869. It became part of the U.S. Constitution on March 30, 1870.

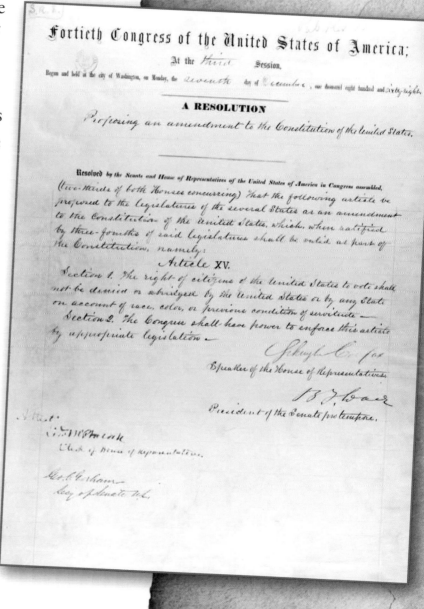

Grant was popular with the American people. So in 1872, the **Republican** Party renominated him for president. They selected Massachusetts senator Henry Wilson for vice president. Grant easily beat **Democratic** candidate Horace Greeley. Greeley's **running mate** was Benjamin Gratz Brown.

President Grant's second term was difficult. Many of the people he trusted took part in **scandals**. His personal secretary, Orville E. Babcock, was involved in the Whiskey Ring. This group cheated the government out of tax money.

Grant's **secretary of war** William W. Belknap was charged with taking bribes. Some Republican leaders even formed a company to steal money from the Union Pacific Railroad. Though he was not involved in these scandals, Grant's reputation suffered.

In 1873, a financial panic swept the country. Many farmers joined the Greenback Party. This group wanted Congress to print more paper money called greenbacks. This money had been printed during the **Civil War**. However, it was not backed by gold.

Grant believed more paper money would hurt the **economy**. So, he **vetoed** Congress's bill to print greenbacks. Instead, Congress passed the Specie Resumption Act in 1875. The act made greenbacks redeemable in gold and silver.

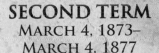

PRESIDENT GRANT'S CABINET

FIRST TERM
MARCH 4, 1869– MARCH 4, 1873

- **STATE –** Elihu B. Washburne
  Hamilton Fish (from March 17, 1869)
- **TREASURY –** George S. Boutwell
- **WAR –** John A. Rawlins
  William T. Sherman (from September 11, 1869)
  William W. Belknap (from November 1, 1869)
- **NAVY –** Adolph E. Borie
  George M. Robeson (from June 25, 1869)
- **ATTORNEY GENERAL –** Ebenezer R. Hoar
  Amos T. Akerman (from July 8, 1870)
  George H. Williams (from January 10, 1872)
- **INTERIOR –** Jacob D. Cox
  Columbus Delano (from November 1, 1870)

SECOND TERM
MARCH 4, 1873– MARCH 4, 1877

- **STATE –** Hamilton Fish
- **TREASURY –** William A. Richardson
  Benjamin H. Bristow (from June 4, 1874)
  Lot M. Morrill (from July 7, 1876)
- **WAR –** William W. Belknap
  Alphonso Taft (from March 11, 1876)
  James D. Cameron (from June 1, 1876)
- **NAVY –** George M. Robeson
- **ATTORNEY GENERAL –** George H. Williams
  Edward Pierrepont (from May 15, 1875)
  Alphonso Taft (from June 1, 1876)
- **INTERIOR –** Columbus Delano
  Zachariah Chandler (from October 19, 1875)

AROUND THE WORLD

Some **Republicans** wanted Grant to run for a third term. But, he did not want to be president again. Grant and his family left the White House in March 1877.

In May, the Grants departed on a trip around the world. Everywhere they went, people cheered. They called Grant the leader who kept America together. The Grants visited many countries in Europe. They also went to Africa, the Middle East, India, and Asia.

After two years, the Grants returned to the United States. Grant was still popular with Americans. Some Republicans hoped to nominate him for president again. But, Grant did not have enough support to be nominated for office. So, he retired from public life.

The family had little money left after their travels. Grant had to sell his army swords to earn extra income. Then, he invested his money in a banking firm. The business failed, and the Grants went broke.

The Grants enjoyed traveling around the world. They saw many new places and met many new people.

Grant kept searching for ways to provide for his family. During this time, he found out he had throat **cancer**. He wanted his family to have enough money after he died. So, he decided to write an **autobiography**. Author Mark Twain was a good friend of Grant's. He agreed to publish Grant's book.

Though ill, Grant worked hard on his autobiography. He finished it shortly before his death. Ulysses S. Grant died on July 23, 1885. He was just 63 years old.

The nation was saddened by Grant's death. Thousands of Americans attended his funeral procession in New York City, New York. Grant was buried in a tomb overlooking the Hudson River. In 1959, his burial site became a national memorial. The General Grant National Memorial is often called Grant's Tomb.

Grant's book, *Personal Memoirs*, was published after his death. It made enough money to support his family for the rest of their lives. It also became one of the best war accounts ever written. Ulysses S. Grant had a challenging presidency. Yet, he remains one of the nation's greatest military heroes.

Grant's Tomb in New York City, New York

OFFICE OF THE PRESIDENT

BRANCHES OF GOVERNMENT

The U.S. government is divided into three branches. They are the executive, legislative, and judicial branches. This division is called a separation of powers. Each branch has some power over the others. This is called a system of checks and balances.

EXECUTIVE BRANCH

The executive branch enforces laws. It is made up of the president, the vice president, and the president's cabinet. The president represents the United States around the world. He or she oversees relations with other countries and signs treaties. The president signs bills into law and appoints officials and federal judges. He or she also leads the military and manages government workers.

LEGISLATIVE BRANCH

The legislative branch makes laws, maintains the military, and regulates trade. It also has the power to declare war. This branch consists of the Senate and the House of Representatives. Together, these two houses make up Congress. Each state has two senators. A state's population determines the number of representatives it has.

JUDICIAL BRANCH

The judicial branch interprets laws. It consists of district courts, courts of appeals, and the Supreme Court. District courts try cases. If a person disagrees with a trial's outcome, he or she may appeal. If the courts of appeals support the ruling, a person may appeal to the Supreme Court. The Supreme Court also makes sure that laws follow the U.S. Constitution.

Qualifications for Office

To be president, a person must meet three requirements. A candidate must be at least 35 years old and a natural-born U.S. citizen. He or she must also have lived in the United States for at least 14 years.

Electoral College

The U.S. presidential election is an indirect election. Voters from each state choose electors to represent them in the Electoral College. The number of electors from each state is based on population. Each elector has one electoral vote. Electors are pledged to cast their vote for the candidate who receives the highest number of popular votes in their state. A candidate must receive the majority of Electoral College votes to win.

Term of Office

Each president may be elected to two four-year terms. Sometimes, a president may only be elected once. This happens if he or she served more than two years of the previous president's term.

The presidential election is held on the Tuesday after the first Monday in November. The president is sworn in on January 20 of the following year. At that time, he or she takes the oath of office:

I do solemnly swear (or affirm) that I will faithfully execute the office of President of the United States, and will to the best of my ability, preserve, protect and defend the Constitution of the United States.

LINE OF SUCCESSION

The Presidential Succession Act of 1947 defines who becomes president if the president cannot serve. The vice president is first in the line of succession. Next are the Speaker of the House and the President Pro Tempore of the Senate. If none of these individuals is able to serve, the office falls to the president's cabinet members. They would take office in the order in which each department was created:

Secretary of State

Secretary of the Treasury

Secretary of Defense

Attorney General

Secretary of the Interior

Secretary of Agriculture

Secretary of Commerce

Secretary of Labor

Secretary of Health and Human Services

Secretary of Housing and Urban Development

Secretary of Transportation

Secretary of Energy

Secretary of Education

Secretary of Veterans Affairs

Secretary of Homeland Security

BENEFITS

- While in office, the president receives a salary of $400,000 each year. He or she lives in the White House and has 24-hour Secret Service protection.

- The president may travel on a Boeing 747 jet called Air Force One. The airplane can accommodate 70 passengers. It has kitchens, a dining room, sleeping areas, and a conference room. It also has fully equipped offices with the latest communications systems. Air Force One can fly halfway around the world before needing to refuel. It can even refuel in flight!

- If the president wishes to travel by car, he or she uses Cadillac One. Cadillac One is a Cadillac Deville. It has been modified with heavy armor and communications systems. The president takes Cadillac One along when visiting other countries if secure transportation will be needed.

- The president also travels on a helicopter called Marine One. Like the presidential car, Marine One accompanies the president when traveling abroad if necessary.

- Sometimes, the president needs to get away and relax with family and friends. Camp David is the official presidential retreat. It is located in the cool, wooded mountains in Maryland. The U.S. Navy maintains the retreat, and the U.S. Marine Corps keeps it secure. The camp offers swimming, tennis, golf, and hiking.

- When the president leaves office, he or she receives Secret Service protection for ten more years. He or she also receives a yearly pension of $191,300 and funding for office space, supplies, and staff.

PRESIDENTS AND THEIR TERMS

PRESIDENT	PARTY	TOOK OFFICE	LEFT OFFICE	TERMS SERVED	VICE PRESIDENT
George Washington	None	April 30, 1789	March 4, 1797	Two	John Adams
John Adams	Federalist	March 4, 1797	March 4, 1801	One	Thomas Jefferson
Thomas Jefferson	Democratic-Republican	March 4, 1801	March 4, 1809	Two	Aaron Burr, George Clinton
James Madison	Democratic-Republican	March 4, 1809	March 4, 1817	Two	George Clinton, Elbridge Gerry
James Monroe	Democratic-Republican	March 4, 1817	March 4, 1825	Two	Daniel D. Tompkins
John Quincy Adams	Democratic-Republican	March 4, 1825	March 4, 1829	One	John C. Calhoun
Andrew Jackson	Democrat	March 4, 1829	March 4, 1837	Two	John C. Calhoun, Martin Van Buren
Martin Van Buren	Democrat	March 4, 1837	March 4, 1841	One	Richard M. Johnson
William H. Harrison	Whig	March 4, 1841	April 4, 1841	Died During First Term	John Tyler
John Tyler	Whig	April 6, 1841	March 4, 1845	Completed Harrison's Term	Office Vacant
James K. Polk	Democrat	March 4, 1845	March 4, 1849	One	George M. Dallas
Zachary Taylor	Whig	March 5, 1849	July 9, 1850	Died During First Term	Millard Fillmore

PRESIDENT	PARTY	TOOK OFFICE	LEFT OFFICE	TERMS SERVED	VICE PRESIDENT
Millard Fillmore	Whig	July 10, 1850	March 4, 1853	Completed Taylor's Term	Office Vacant
Franklin Pierce	Democrat	March 4, 1853	March 4, 1857	One	William R.D. King
James Buchanan	Democrat	March 4, 1857	March 4, 1861	One	John C. Breckinridge
Abraham Lincoln	Republican	March 4, 1861	April 15, 1865	Served One Term, Died During Second Term	Hannibal Hamlin, Andrew Johnson
Andrew Johnson	Democrat	April 15, 1865	March 4, 1869	Completed Lincoln's Second Term	Office Vacant
Ulysses S. Grant	Republican	March 4, 1869	March 4, 1877	Two	Schuyler Colfax, Henry Wilson
Rutherford B. Hayes	Republican	March 3, 1877	March 4, 1881	One	William A. Wheeler
James A. Garfield	Republican	March 4, 1881	September 19, 1881	Died During First Term	Chester Arthur
Chester Arthur	Republican	September 20, 1881	March 4, 1885	Completed Garfield's Term	Office Vacant
Grover Cleveland	Democrat	March 4, 1885	March 4, 1889	One	Thomas A. Hendricks
Benjamin Harrison	Republican	March 4, 1889	March 4, 1893	One	Levi P. Morton
Grover Cleveland	Democrat	March 4, 1893	March 4, 1897	One	Adlai E. Stevenson
William McKinley	Republican	March 4, 1897	September 14, 1901	Served One Term, Died During Second Term	Garret A. Hobart, Theodore Roosevelt

PRESIDENT	PARTY	TOOK OFFICE	LEFT OFFICE	TERMS SERVED	VICE PRESIDENT
Theodore Roosevelt	Republican	September 14, 1901	March 4, 1909	Completed McKinley's Second Term, Served One Term	Office Vacant, Charles Fairbanks
William Taft	Republican	March 4, 1909	March 4, 1913	One	James S. Sherman
Woodrow Wilson	Democrat	March 4, 1913	March 4, 1921	Two	Thomas R. Marshall
Warren G. Harding	Republican	March 4, 1921	August 2, 1923	Died During First Term	Calvin Coolidge
Calvin Coolidge	Republican	August 3, 1923	March 4, 1929	Completed Harding's Term, Served One Term	Office Vacant, Charles Dawes
Herbert Hoover	Republican	March 4, 1929	March 4, 1933	One	Charles Curtis
Franklin D. Roosevelt	Democrat	March 4, 1933	April 12, 1945	Served Three Terms, Died During Fourth Term	John Nance Garner, Henry A. Wallace, Harry S. Truman
Harry S. Truman	Democrat	April 12, 1945	January 20, 1953	Completed Roosevelt's Fourth Term, Served One Term	Office Vacant, Alben Barkley
Dwight D. Eisenhower	Republican	January 20, 1953	January 20, 1961	Two	Richard Nixon
John F. Kennedy	Democrat	January 20, 1961	November 22, 1963	Died During First Term	Lyndon B. Johnson
Lyndon B. Johnson	Democrat	November 22, 1963	January 20, 1969	Completed Kennedy's Term, Served One Term	Office Vacant, Hubert H. Humphrey
Richard Nixon	Republican	January 20, 1969	August 9, 1974	Completed First Term, Resigned During Second Term	Spiro T. Agnew, Gerald Ford

PRESIDENTS 26–37, 1901–1974

PRESIDENT	PARTY	TOOK OFFICE	LEFT OFFICE	TERMS SERVED	VICE PRESIDENT
Gerald Ford	Republican	August 9, 1974	January 20, 1977	Completed Nixon's Second Term	Nelson A. Rockefeller
Jimmy Carter	Democrat	January 20, 1977	January 20, 1981	One	Walter Mondale
Ronald Reagan	Republican	January 20, 1981	January 20, 1989	Two	George H.W. Bush
George H.W. Bush	Republican	January 20, 1989	January 20, 1993	One	Dan Quayle
Bill Clinton	Democrat	January 20, 1993	January 20, 2001	Two	Al Gore
George W. Bush	Republican	January 20, 2001	January 20, 2009	Two	Dick Cheney
Barack Obama	Democrat	January 20, 2009			Joe Biden

"Let us have peace." Ulysses S. Grant

WRITE TO THE PRESIDENT

You may write to the president at:

**The White House
1600 Pennsylvania Avenue NW
Washington, DC 20500**

You may e-mail the president at:

comments@whitehouse.gov

GLOSSARY

amendment - a change to a country's constitution.

annex - to take land and add it to a nation.

assassinate - to murder a very important person, usually for political reasons.

autobiography - a story of a person's life that is written by himself or herself.

barrack - a building or set of buildings used for housing soldiers.

brevet - a military title given to an officer who has a higher rank than he or she is paid for.

cadet - a student in a military academy.

cancer - any of a group of often deadly diseases characterized by an abnormal growth of cells that destroys healthy tissues and organs.

civil war - a war between groups in the same country. The United States of America and the Confederate States of America fought a civil war from 1861 to 1865.

Confederate States of America - the country formed by the states of South Carolina, Georgia, Florida, Alabama, Louisiana, Mississippi, Texas, Virginia, Tennessee, Arkansas, and North Carolina when they left the Union between 1860 and 1861. It is also called the Confederacy.

Constitution - the laws that govern the United States. Something relating to or following the laws of a constitution is constitutional.

Democrat - a member of the Democratic political party. When Ulysses S. Grant was president, Democrats supported farmers and landowners.

economy - the way a nation uses its money, goods, and natural resources.

financier (fih-nuhn-SIHR)- a person skilled in financial matters, such as a banker.

infantry - soldiers trained and organized to fight on foot.

real estate - property, which includes buildings and land.

Reconstruction - the period after the American Civil War when laws were passed to help the Southern states rebuild and return to the Union.

regiment - a large military unit made up of troops.

Republican - a member of the Republican political party. When Ulysses S. Grant was president, Republicans supported business and strong government.

running mate - a candidate running for a lower-rank position on an election ticket, especially the candidate for vice president.

scandal - an action that shocks people and disgraces those connected with it.

secretary of war - a member of the president's cabinet who handles the nation's defense.

Speaker of the House - the highest-ranking member of the party with the majority in Congress.

tanner - a person whose business is tanning hides. Tanning is the process of changing hides into leather.

treasury - a place where money is kept.

veto - the right of one member of a decision-making group to stop an action by the group. In the U.S. government, the president can veto bills passed by Congress. But Congress can override the president's veto if two-thirds of its members vote to do so.

WEB SITES

To learn more about Ulysses S. Grant, visit ABDO Publishing Company on the World Wide Web at **www.abdopublishing.com**. Web sites about Ulysses S. Grant are featured on our Book Links page. These links are routinely monitored and updated to provide the most current information available.

INDEX